An Elephant Grows Up

by Anastasia Suen ~ illustrated by Michael L. Denman and William J. Huiett

Thanks to our advisers for their expertise, research, and advice:

Larry Killmar, Deputy Director of Collections
Zoological Society of San Diego
San Diego Zoo
San Diego, California

Susan Kesselring, M.A., Literacy Educator
Rosemount–Apple Valley–Eagan (Minnesota) School District

Editorial Director: Carol Jones
Managing Editor: Catherine Neitge
Creative Director: Keith Griffin
Editor: Christianne Jones
Story Consultant: Terry Flaherty
Designer: Nathan Gassman
Production Artist: Angela Kilmer
Page Production: Picture Window Books
The illustrations in this book were created with acrylics.

Picture Window Books
5115 Excelsior Boulevard, Suite 232
Minneapolis, MN 55416
877-845-8392
www.picturewindowbooks.com

Printed in the United States of America.

Library of Congress Cataloging-in-Publication Data
Suen, Anastasia.
An elephant grows up / by Anastasia Suen ; illustrated by Michael Denman and
William J. Huiett.
p. cm. — (Wild animals)
Includes bibliographical references and index.
ISBN 1-4048-0984-8 (hardcover)
ISBN 1-4048-1802-2 (paperback)
1. Elephants—Infancy—Juvenile literature. 2. Elephants—Development—Juvenile
literature. I. Denman, Michael L., ill. II. Huiett, William J., 1943- ill. III. Title.
QL737.P98S84 2006
599.67'139—dc22
2005004283

Welcome to the world of wild animals! Follow a baby elephant and her brother as they grow up under the hot African sun. As they become adults, they separate and have their own families.

Under the hot African sun, a baby elephant is born. The calf looks small next to her mother, but she weighs more than a refrigerator!

A female elephant is called a cow. A male is called a bull.

Less than an hour after birth,
the elephant calf can stand.
She is already taller than
your kitchen table!

The calf is hungry, so she nuzzles up to her mother to drink milk.

Calves are covered in hair when they are born. Older elephants only have long hair at the ends of their tails.

Mothers and their young stay together in one herd. Young adult males and older males roam by themselves or join small herds of other males.

The herd stays in one place for several days after the calf is born. Once the new calf can walk, the herd will move on.

Elephants often walk in single file lines along the trails. The calves walk behind or next to their mothers.

Looking for food is a full-time job for elephants. They spend about 16 hours a day eating. They only sleep a few hours a day.

The oldest cow in the herd leads the other elephants. She traveled these same trails when she was a calf.

11

The long trail leads the elephants to a
popular gathering place—the water hole.
They visit the water hole at least once a day.

At first, the calf uses her mouth to drink the water. As she grows older, the calf learns how to use her trunk. She sucks water into her trunk and then blows it into her mouth.

An elephant's trunk is the elephant's nose and upper lip. Some young elephants suck their trunks like babies suck their thumbs.

The calf grows up fast. She begins to eat plants like the older elephants. She also uses her trunk to grab leaves high in the trees.

Mothers nurse their calves for about two years. Only after the mother stops nursing will she have another baby.

The calf uses her tusks to dig for water. Some elephants use their right tusk more. Other elephants prefer their left tusk. It's just like being right-handed or left-handed.

A new surprise has arrived in the herd. At four years old, the calf now has a baby brother! When full grown, male elephants are much larger than female.

African elephants are the largest land animals.

Calves soon start to use their tusks for more than just digging. They use their tusks for resting their heavy trunks or ripping bark off trees. The tusks can also be used as weapons when needed.

The brother and sister have grown a lot, but they are still growing. Most elephants keep growing until they are 30 or 40 years old!

When the brother is about nine years old, he will join a different herd. The sister will stay with the cows and the calves in her herd and start a family.

Bulls and cows live apart. At mating time, they call one another with low sounds that humans cannot hear.

The elephant family continues
to grow. The calf grew up and became a
mother herself. She is now called a cow.

Her brother also started a family in a different herd. He is now called a bull. A new journey begins under the hot African sun.

A mother elephant always watches over her calf to make sure all is well.

Elephant Diagram

① **EARS** Elephants have their own air conditioning. As elephants flap their ears, the blood flow cools their body down.

② **FEET** Although an elephant can weigh between 8,000 and 12,000 pounds (3,600 and 5,400 kilograms), they can walk in complete silence. They rarely leave footprints.

③ **SKIN** An elephant's skin is very sensitive. In fact, an elephant can feel a small fly landing on its skin.

④ **TRUNK** The trunk of an elephant is the longest nose of any living animal.

⑤ **TUSKS** Tusks are no different than ordinary teeth.

Map

Wild elephants can be found in Africa and Asia.
The elephants in this book are from Africa.

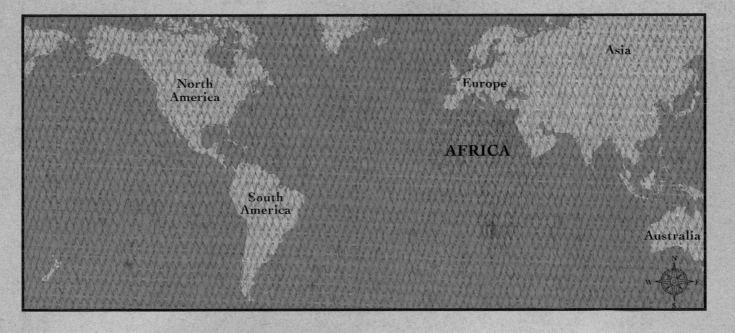

Glossary

bull—a male elephant

calf—a young elephant

cow—a female elephant

herd—a group of animals that live together

nurse—to drink milk from the mother

trunk—the elephant's long nose and upper lip

tusks—long, pointed teeth that stick out of the elephant's mouth

To Learn More

At the Library

Hanson, Adners. *Elephants Are Not Little!* Edina, Minn.: ABDO Pub., 2005.
Kulling, Monica. *Elephants: Life in the Wild.* New York: Golden Books, 2000.
Lantier, Patricia, and Anthony D. Fredericks. *The Wonder of Elephants.*
    Milwaukee: Gareth Stevens Pub., 2001.

On the Web

FactHound offers a safe, fun way to find Web
sites related to this book. All of the sites on
FactHound have been researched by our staff.

1. Visit *www.facthound.com*

2. Type in this special code: 1404809848

3. Click on the FETCH IT button.

Your trusty FactHound will fetch the best sites for you!

Index

Look for all of the books in the Wild Animals series:

A Baboon Grows Up   A Rhinoceros Grows Up

A Hippopotamus Grows Up   A Tiger Grows Up

A Lion Grows Up   An Elephant Grows Up